The Jungle Gospel

The Inner Architect of Reality

James Gain

Ripple Logic™

Ripple Ministry™

August 1986

Ripple Legacy Press™
Chicago, Illinois

Published by Ripple❦Legacy Press™
Chicago, Illinois

https://ripple-logic.com

Library of Congress Cataloging-in-Publication Data
Gain, James.
The Jungle Gospel: the inner architect of reality
James Gain.   pages cm. (Ripple Ministry Series; book one)
Includes bibliographical references.

I. Title. II. Series: Ripple Ministry Series ; bk. 1.
BV4501.3 .G35 2026 — 248.4—dc23

ISBN: 979-8-9936851-3-7 — paperback
ISBN: 979-8-9936851-2-0 — e-book

Printed in the United States of America.
First Edition
English

RIPPLE MINISTRY

Book Series

Book One: The Jungle Gospel

Book Two: [reserved]

Book Three: [reserved]

DISCLAIMER

The contents of these works are drawn from the author's personal private journals collection and is shared for reflection and personal enrichment. These works do not offer any form of guidance for mental health, legal matters nor financial decisions, or any other professional domains. All readers are solely responsible for their own choices, interpretations, and actions. The author assumes no liability for any outcomes resulting from the use or misuse of this material.

Contents

ACKNOWLEDGMENTS

To the ancient supercentenarian teacher and the wise people who crossed my path, long before I even understood I was on an eternal journey. As a young seeker I carried a knowing and quiet ache inside of me, a sense of something calling, but I didn't know its name yet.

Across more than forty years of practice and decades of studies around the world…, through Vietnam, and Asia, Turkey, Azerbaijan, Armenia, Egypt, Afghanistan, Greece, India, Tibet, Japan, Europe, Russia., and more than 37 countries. There were many people who helped me develop wisdom and understanding on this narrow path.

Some offered me complex wisdom through stories that were passed down through many… eons of generations. Others shared simple disciplines with structure and the kind of guidance that reshapes your life from the inside out. A few taught me…., with profound silence, the kind that reaches into your inner world rearranging everything you thought you knew, but didn't.

There were moments when a single gesture, a glance or a sentence spoken in alignment, would open doors I had known existed. There were months spent in monasteries high up on mountainsides, in faraway temples and hard to reach caves. And jungles — of fun. Kitchen tables and secluded trainings, where the wisdom became understanding, that arrived like a quiet moment — before the dawn.

The kind that embraces your face with your hand.

These teachers knew I was coming to them, long before I had considered a journey to go there. They recognized light and something rare in me — long before I even had the courage to claim it.

They gave me knowledge and tools of wisdom to get understanding — of the inner workings of what I had been doing instinctively… since — childhood. They offered me a language that is never spoken… because words cannot contain — that wisdom. They each offered me direction for the restlessness I had always felt. And grounding for those parts of me… still learning how to master my own natural abilities. Yeah…, Monk… L. O. L.

This book carries… many of their rare presence and gifts of understanding within all of these works. Their fingerprints dwell in the very framework…, of this architecture. Echoes of their boundless generosity is forever etched through these very pages.

To every conscious soul of wisdom — I've ever had the honor of meeting, wherever you are now, thank you. For shaping the seeker you found, into the teacher I've become. You shone the light of eternal wisdom upon me, with kind mercy. And grace has given its understanding for those roots to grow.

My eternal gratitude
James

DEDICATION

A Prayer for the Brokenhearted

Father, this little book is dedicated to those who carry quiet burdens and to the ones whose hearts have been bruised by loss, disappointment, or loneliness.

To those who feel unseen… unheard, or unsure of their next step and those who have prayed through tears, or wondered if hope still belongs to them.

Let Your comforts… reach those places no one else can touch, and let your peace settle the storms they cannot calm. May your love remind them, they're not abandoned…. never overlooked, never beyond your healing. Might these pages…. gently guide them toward the one who restores, renews, and makes all things new.

Amen.

Scripture:
"The Lord is near unto them
that are of a broken heart…" — **Psalm 34:18**

THE BIBLE MATTERS

For a book that has been written across — thousands of years and many diffcrent cultures…, by shepherds, kings, fishermen, and prophets. The Bible is., an interesting and surprisingly unified message. People have often debated its doctrines, its history, and interpretations — but when you zoom out, a very clear story emerges from its core.

It's a story about God and us.
These two realities intertwined together.

What follows is my own simple conversational walk with God and how his words changed my life, with the Bible's most important ideas, that I recalled from memorized verses.

The "Core message"
that changed my life forever.

Author's Note

This book was born out of my own long journey through hardships. In the darkest seasons of my life. These scriptures became my lifeline — a quiet voice reminding me God is always here with us. My hope is that this story might offer you the same peace and comfort it has brought me.

If this book helps you then please share.

Find yourself a Bible…, start reading the books of psalms and proverbs. Those two books brought me comfort and peace of mind through many hardships.

Let hope by salvation ripple forward.

INTRODUCTION

I didn't write this book to teach you anything. I wrote it to show you something that happened to me in 1986. A moment that cracked open the world I thought I understood and revealed the fabric of reality I had carried inside of me since childhood. That very same reality Jesus' spoke of with absolute clarity:

"The kingdom of heaven is within you."

For years, I didn't know what that meant. I had no idea of how to actually see this place. I didn't know... how to walk in it.

But life has a way of preparing you long before you realize you're being prepared. Verses I learned as a child, instincts I couldn't explain, and moments of intuition that made no sense at the time. It was all leading me toward a single moment, in a jungle on the far side of the world.

A moment that would change everything. This book isn't about religion. It isn't about doctrine. It isn't about convincing you of anything. It's about awareness. It's about identity. It's about the kingdom within — the one Jesus described. The one most people never learn to see, the one that opened inside of me, in a way I could never forget.

I'm not asking you to believe my story. I'm inviting you to recognize — your own. Because if you're holding this book, something in you is already stirring. Something is already waking up. Something is already — reaching for the truth that has been inside of you… since the beginning. This is my story, but the kingdom is yours too.

Peace, Love, and Light.
James

Companion Videos

BEFORE YOU READ

This journal entry comes from a — profound moment in my life when intuition, trust, and the raw power woven into the fabric of creation didn't whisper…. they hit me with a force I couldn't step away from. Not with gentle nudges. No quiet suggestions. Pure unfiltered truth that stripped me down to what's real and left me standing there with no excuses.

Where every heartbeat carried a kind of animal awareness, the kind that climbs up your spine — and sharpens your instincts. You know you're not alone, you can't name it, but you feel it making every step more brutally honest.

I'm not writing all of it down — some of it lived on the edge. But this moment stayed with me. Something was moving through me and around us. It didn't care about plans, training, or bravado. It demanded my full undivided and complete attention.

I'm sharing this moment with you because this is where everything I thought I understood — cracked open and something deeper, older, more powerful… than creation itself stepped forward; raw, primal and uncompromising. A moment that asked one question with absolute clarity:

Who are you going to be, from this moment on.?

THE
JUNGLE
GOSPEL

FROM THE 1986
NARROW PATH JOURNAL

1

July 1972
Narrow Path
Begins

My internal awareness began around age seven. I didn't know the meaning of many words, but I could feel spirit. I had a natural intuition even back then. The word kingdom was a mystery — I thought it meant castles, stone walls, maybe a moat. Something out there, not in here.

Intuition wasn't dramatic or mystical…, it was quiet like the kind that settles into a child before the adults lie and teach them how to be stupid and ignore it.

Sometimes it comes as a feeling, like the air around me is shifting, with a knowing that doesn't need proof. Sometimes it would be a verse I'd memorized but didn't fully understand or recognize would get into alignment.

"…keep my words… write them in your heart…"

I didn't know how important… Proverbs 7 really was, because I didn't know…, it was wisdom itself. I just knew it felt true. Adults around me called it my imagination and teachers said I was daydreaming. But I knew better.

Something inside of me was listening and learning truth for the world I was already being prepared for by — age 7. A moment that I wouldn't experience… until decades later in a jungle on the far side of the world.

When everything I thought I understood would collapse and be reborn into something new, in a single breath.

At seven years old, all I knew was this:

There was more to the world than what I could see, and not all adults speak truth, many of them lied. Somehow this knowingness was already speaking to me through intuitional awareness.

When I was about ten years old, I had an experience in Sunday school that ended up shaping more of my life than I realized at the time. We used these little printed lesson booklets, and each week the teacher assigned the next section for us to study at home. I actually enjoyed that part because it let me learn at my own pace.

But the class itself was unpredictable. Some Sundays the teacher showed up late—sometimes half an hour or more. Other times he didn't show up at all, and we'd just talk about whatever came to mind instead of what we had studied. The moment that changed everything was the morning he walked in still hungover from the night before. Even as kids, we knew that wasn't right. I told him he might want to go sleep it off, and he left.

The rest of the class looked at me and decided I should take over as the substitute teacher. For a ten-year-old, that was a big moment. Thankfully, I had actually done the reading. From then on, our studies were solid, our discussions were meaningful, and we enjoyed the class a whole lot more.

A few months later, he returned with a testimony about giving up drinking and getting help through a counseling program. That was good to hear. I kept teaching the class for the next few years, and in that time, I picked up a lot of small but important lessons—little pieces of wisdom that would become guiding lights later in my life.

2

Verses That Followed Me

Some people memorize Scriptures…., I did it every day. Those scriptures began to live in me. Certain verses attached themselves to my life early, not as rules or doctrine but as companions through all of the… brutality of my childhood. They surfaced in quiet moments, in hard moments — and times when I didn't even know what I needed until the words arrived. These verses became the seeds of my inner world:

"…for God so loved the world…"
"…God is always Faithful…"
"Ask and it shall be given to you"

I didn't understand all of their full weight yet…, But I felt them. They weren't just scriptures or empty promises. They were simple truths steady…, unchanging. And they carried something else with them, a promise that there was a way through this human experience and the brokenness, and the onslaught of life.

I didn't know it then, but these verses were forming the architecture of my inner life and they were threads that would later pull me through a strange dark transformative moment in my life.

They were preparing me for this… narrow path journey long before I even knew I was walking it.

3

JOURNEY TO THE JUNGLE

God has — a way of shaping you long before you realize you need shaping. By the time I reached adulthood those early sparks of intuition, the verses, and the quiet knowing, had all woven themselves into the background of my life. I didn't talk about this much. I didn't have the language for it yet. But it was there, guiding me in ways I did not fully understand.

I learned discipline, structure and how to survive in environments that demanded strength, precision and focus. But beneath all of that… something else was growing, a deeper awareness and sense that the world wasn't just physical, and that reality was not limited… to what you could touch or measure.

"…draw near to God, and He will draw near to you"

Sometimes, a verse would surface at the oddest moment: other times it was just a feeling… a nudge, or a whisper that didn't come from thought. I didn't know it then, but I was being led towards a moment that would tear the floor out from underneath of my reality. A moment that would collapse my old world and instantly create a new one. A moment that would fuse everything I had learned, every verse, every instinct, every spark into this — undeniable truth. 1986 wasn't waiting for me. It was calling me. And I was walking straight towards it.

4

THE

JUNGLE

The jungle was hot, humid and sticky, like wearing a second skin that didn't belong to you. It was…, pressing into our consciousness, thick and heavy. You could feel it everywhere, a sensation raising all of your goosebumps without offering a reason. The air tasted like mildew, sweat, and some old forgotten bar rag. There really is no language to describe how gross it all actually felt.

Tom was ahead of me, our boots sinking into the gooey muck. He was always muttering something again, always something. About the heat or bugs. I barely listened to him anymore. My senses were stretched too thin, tuned into — something else I couldn't quite name. Every step felt like I was being watched, not by eyes, but by something as old as the world itself. And somewhere in the back of my mind, a familiar verse surfaced:

"The kingdom of heaven
is within you"

It wasn't a thought; it was a presence, a memory rising like an echo through a canyon. A verse I'd carried since childhood, tucked into that quiet place in the depth of my heart. It always intrigued me, even though I never fully understood it. But it gave me comfort.

We kept on walking; our feet were killing us. It was nearly impossible to see anything. The jungle canopy was choking out the sun like a pro-wrestler.

The ground beneath of us was growing darker, wetter and stranger. The jungle had a way of making you feel small, not in a fearful way; but in a way that reminded you, that you were only a temporary guest in something ancient.

Tom cracked a joke about dying out there. I didn't laugh, as a few verses were flickering through my mind… softly, but sharp:

> ***"Though I walk through the valley
> of the shadow of death…"***

> ***"For all have sinned"***

> ***"Ask anything of your father in heaven
> and he will give it to you"***

Not condemnation, just some recognition and gentle reminder of the human condition. The fragility of life and the ego-mind, the way fear tries to rewrite the story before the truth even has a chance to speak.

We kept moving, by the time night fell — we were even more lost; not metaphorically, not spiritually, but really physically undeniably lost. No rendezvous point. No bearings and no light.

Just two men in a jungle with something ancient, that didn't care about plans, training or bravado. And yet… beneath the fear, exhaustion and rising panic, something else was stirring … something I'd known since I was seven.

There it was again; Proverbs chapter seven, the one that had carved itself into me a long time before I could even understand why:

Wisdom wasn't some vague concept out there...., It was something alive in here. And that's when the shift really began; subtle at first, like the air changing before a storm.

I didn't know it yet, but the old world I was living in was beginning to fracture. The collapse had already begun.

These verses I'd carried for fourteen years, the ones I had repeated in the quiet moments — of my life in my mind, were about to become — the only solid ground beneath my feet.

5

THE
JUNGLE
CONTINUED

Those next several days blurred together — with snakes, bugs, and every miserable thing the bush could throw at us. The jungle wasn't just a place anymore; it was a presence with pressure. "A mirror of our mouths and imaginations".

Somewhere in the middle of all that heat and exhaustion, I felt it happen, something inside of me snapped into focus. It hit me quietly at first. A realization rising from the edges of my awareness, — we weren't just walking into these situations blindly. We were actually creating them. Every fear, complaint, expectations and stupid… careless word. They weren't random thoughts, they were… instructions, shaping what was coming next with unnerving precision.

Right there in the middle of that realization these verses hit me like lightning:

> ***"Ask anything of your Father in heaven, and it shall be given to you"***

> ***"Seek ye first the kingdom of heaven, and all these things will be added to you"***

And the verses that ring like bells in my mind ever since that moment.

> ***"In the beginning was the word and the word was with GOD and the word was GOD"***

> ***"Guard your tongue"***

14

These verses didn't arrive as bible theology they arrived as truth; sharp, alive and undeniably true.

Then another verse surfaced, one I hadn't thought of in years, because some idiot deleted it from the new bible I carried with me always. <u>Mathew 17:21</u> & Mark 9:29

"But this kind comes only by prayer and fasting"

I had not eaten a real meal in a few days, and we're both about out of safe water. I was walking with God, praying in my mind, in my heart and on my lips, with every step, every breath, every heartbeat. My body was empty, my mind was focused, and my spirit was wide open.

And that's when it happened.
The collapse. The detonation. The shift.

I didn't bother explaining any of it., to Tom. I was pissed off at him anyway. Sorry Tom. I just stopped… right there in the middle of that wet, sticky gooey muck, and turned to Tom and said:

"**Tom**, I imagine we'll be back in camp tonight. Hot meal. Long shower. Soft cot. No bugs or Tigers"

He laughed — that nervous ego-mind laugh people use when they are afraid to believe… something bigger than themselves., or their Ego—mind had them in a tail spin. He muttered something about us dying out there…. and these verses popped into my head. REALLY — SHARP.

"Your tongue plots destruction
like a sharp razor."

"a false tongue hates a clean heart"
"Guard your tongue"

I shrugged and said "Well Tom that's just as possible as my idea…; but I like mine better. So, let's go with that."

He snorted. "And how the hell are we going to find our way back?" I said the first thing that popped in my mind, half sarcasm but 100% intuition and instinct:

"I don't know…, TOM… Maybe a snake will drop out of a tree in front of us and say, 'Follow me.'"

Five seconds later, not exaggerating… a big snake drops right in front of us, hitting the ground with a heavy thud and hissing…, then it lifted its head, looking back toward us, like it was checking to see if the two idiots are paying attention… and then it slithered off slowly at a left angle. We just stared at it, for about three seconds.

Then I looked at Tom. "There we go," I said.

He didn't laugh this time. He didn't say… a word. He just followed me and the snake, shaking his head.

I trailed that big snake for about half a kilometer, maybe more. Then it suddenly changed direction…, bolting off fast and disappearing into the dense undergrowth. My mind was sensing everything, on a higher level.

Tom exhaled hard. "Now what?"

"Shut up Tom," I said. "Listen."

And there it was — faint, but real. A small motor running, somewhere in the distance. I just looked at Tom.

I followed that motor sound until we saw sunlight shining through the trees. We reached a narrow backwater canal, where we saw this tiny Thai man…., sitting in a little boat piled high with vegetation. Tom's mouth hung open like he was looking at a ghost. The look on his face, was priceless.

We waved and said, the only Thai we knew, help please. Pord chwy dwy. He motioned us to get in. We rode with him until we reached a little dirt path road., then we walked until our feet could not take one more step. Tom finally broke the silence with another complaint, "Now what?"

I didn't hesitate this time, because now I knew.

I said, "Any minute now — a blue truck will stop by, pick us up and take us back to camp." He stared at me.

"Oh yeah? And how do you know that?"

I didn't know how to explain it — I didn't even have the language yet. **"I just know," I said.** He laughed., right as I tapped his shoulder… pointing down the road at a truck that was kicking up dust in the distance. Tom shook his head slowly and all he said was:

"Damn, dude. Just… damn."

A few minutes later… we were crammed in the back of a farmer's truck, bouncing along…, for about half an hour. Then he dropped us off at a main road, about a mile from camp, and one of our own trucks picked us up from there.

Turns out we were AWOL for five days and seventeen miles off course. The commander enjoyed chewing us out, but nothing serious happened. We got our hot meal, shower, soft cot, no bugs or Tigers (much longer story).

I saw Tom, a few more times after that, and we talked about all of it and said we'd keep in touch. Couple of weeks later we rotated out of there, we never did meet again. That was forty years ago. A fond memory now but more importantly it was also the moment everything changed for me. The moment I realized something I couldn't explain yet, but somehow already knew how to do.

And that's really all you need to know anyway:
Just do it.

6

THE
COLLAPSE

Something shifted right before that snake dropped from the tree. Long before the boat, or truck. It began with a realization so quiet I almost missed it: And had it not been for the fact, that we were out in the middle of a jungle, I would have missed it.

I remembered a scripture that tells us to go to our room and close the door. So, we can hear the still small voice that speaks wisdom to us. You know "that was profound" and a moment that would truly live in me for the rest of my life.

We were out there in the middle of a jungle, exactly what it takes to have a transformational experience. Nothing else but survival on your mind; top front and center. Back in the world as we called it, we would talk about nothing much at all; passing time without thinking about anything important. Guess being out in a jungle was a lot better than being eaten by a big fish and barfed up on the shoreline. Like Jonah of Ninevah in the old bible story.

<u>**Our Words**</u>
<u>**were shaping the World around us.**</u>

Good — Bad — Beautiful and Ugly
All of It

"In the beginning was the Word
The Word was with GOD
The Word Was GOD"

That last one made me laugh actually. Kinda was thinking, what did Jonah say before a giant fish swallowed him whole, bet he knew a Tom.

Every fear had become a doorway and complaints a path. And expectations became a blueprint. When that truth hit me, something inside of me snapped; not in a painful way, but in a way that felt like the floor of my inner world of reality gave way and it opened into something much older, deeper, and far more real.

The Bible verses were popping into place like
lightning strikes to my awareness
whenever we said anything.

*"Ask anything of your Father in heaven,
And it shall be given unto you"*

Then another:

*"Seek ye first the kingdom of heaven,
And all these things will be added unto you"*

And then this one sealed it:

**"This kind comes
only by prayer and fasting"**

We hadn't eaten in a few days and
I was walking — in prayer with every step.

My body was fasting
And my mind was sharp and focused,
My spirit was wide open.

In that moment
those verses and reality collided inside of me.,
at the same time that's when the collapse happened.

The old world didn't fall apart with noise.

It fell apart with clarity.

A clarity so sharp that it cut through all fear and doubt
And the ego-mind was subdued in a single breath.

I didn't understand it yet.
But I could feel it.

Something ancient was waking up inside of me.
Something that had been there
all along.

7

A New World is Born

The collapse wasn't the end
It was the ignition point
Like being reborn.

One heartbeat I'm standing in the jungle exhausted, thirsty, hungry with a pounding headache — plus lost. The next heartbeat, everything inside of me inverted.

It felt like the entire architecture of reality folded inward like the polarized fields of existence and then it snapped into alignment like the universe inside of me collapsed into a single point of impossible density.

A silent implosion.
No noise. No thought. No identity.

I felt the intense gravitational pull of it, like something so powerful it's difficult to describe. Sovereign., ancient and demanding my absolute undivided attention.

Then it blew open.

Not softly or symbolically.
But with the sheer force of creation itself
exploding outward
from its core.

A new world erupted from within me.
Violent, precise and undeniable.

I could feel myself resonating within the very fabric of it, as if my awareness had been rewired… directly into the fabric of reality itself.

One, if not "the most" profound moments of my life. And as I look back at those moments now, I realize that was an awakening moment for me. We have all kinds of cool phrases for it now. Back then it felt like power over my own life was granted to me. Along with a full working set of schematics to go along with it.

I've written a lot about this subject for several decades. And for 10 years straight I worked directly with a few selected people that I could see the potential within them and felt inspired to spend the time working with them. At the end of those 10 years only a few actually applied it to their lives and changed anything they wanted.

The others wasted the wisdom and understanding I taught them; exactly as the bible stories had illustrated. Those handpicked students taught me deeper wisdom, that I may not have discovered without having taught those lessons to them for 10 years.

It was life changing and when you see the bigger picture of what was learned in that moment, it will change everything in your life. If you apply that very simple lesson.

Every instinct sharpened
every lie burned away. With every truth illuminated
in that detonation, I understood something profound,
without words:

The old world I had been living in was gone.

Not metaphorically.

Gone

What arose in its place was not insight.
It wasn't wisdom or enlightenment.

It was a new world
one that I recognized instantly, even though
I had never seen it before.

A world that felt perfectly right.

It felt like home.

8

THE KINGDOM WITHIN

When the dust settled inside me, when the collapse and the detonation had done their work, one verse rose up, above all the others, not as memory. Not as a teaching. But as a revelation.

**"Except a man be born again, he cannot see
The kingdom of God."**

I had read it thousands of times and many times heard it preached. I had repeated it in my mind at least ten thousand times since childhood.

But I had never understood it
Not until that moment.

Because suddenly it was no longer a metaphor. It wasn't a Sunday school doctrine… It wasn't even a requirement for heaven someday later. It was a description… of a real place, a real state of beingness, that truly is a real transformation.

A description of what just happened inside of me.

I had been born again.

not into a religion
not into a Bible thumper's belief system.

A completely new perception of reality.

A new awareness was now in my consciousness.

A place I now know
is real.

"With eyes that see. And ears that hear"

And the kingdom of heaven
the one Jesus was saying is *within you*
was suddenly real
and visible.

Not as imagination or symbolism.
But as reality.

A living, breathing, sovereign reality
woven into the fabric of existence, accessible through this
doorway of the inner world.

In that moment, I understood:

Jesus wasn't giving us religious doctrines.

How many times did Jesus repeatedly show us,
exactly how he felt about religions.

He was illustrating and describing how the mechanics of the
soul works, in unison with God's creation.

He was telling us, exactly how reality works
and how the kingdom works
how rebirth works.

And the very best part is, how to walk through life with
the full authority as God designed us to carry
from the very beginning back in
Genesis Chapter 1:27

**The look on my face
must have been priceless.**

**Talk about an ah-ha moment
that one was mine.**

9

RIPPLE ❤ LOGIC™

DISCOVERED

When I returned from the jungle, everything looked different, because I was different. People think of... transformation announcing itself with fireworks or something, well... It doesn't. It arrives quietly — like a new operating system running beneath the surface of your life.

I didn't have a name for it then. I didn't fully understand the mechanics of it yet. I just knew something fundamental had changed. In the way I perceived all of reality.

I could feel the structure behind events. I could sense the ways thoughts moved before they became actions. I could see how emotions shaped outcomes and... I could watch conversations as they rippled outward into consequences. It was like seeing the blueprint on the table before it became something in the world.

Slowly over years of living, observing, and testing what I had experienced in that jungle. I started to realize something that was fundamentally important had occurred.

Reality responds to the inner world
Always, without exception.

Not because we "manifest" anything, because we really don't. Not because we "attract" things. But because the kingdom within us is tied directly to the engine of creation, the place where thought, intention, and spirit intersect in alignment with the fabric of creation. That is what makes our reality; resonance and agreement.

I understood in an instant — the simplistic Logic of this fabric of reality. Every choice, every word and every belief sends out a ripple 🌀 and those ripples shape the world we walk through. That's when the name came to me:

Ripple 🌀 Logic™
Not a philosophy, a description.

How the kingdom within us is interacting with the world around us. A true description of how God designed us to walk; in the authority Jesus taught us how to use.

Ripple Logic… wasn't anything I invented. I simply saw it as something and recognized it, like reading an operating schematic. Because I had been living it in a jungle…. long before I discovered the language to articulate something so intricate as the schematic of creation. Truly inspiring.!

Ripple 🌀 Logic™

Once you see it
you cannot unsee it.

When we lift our eyes to the vast sweep of the heavens, creation itself becomes a testimony — the skies shimmering with the quiet declaration of God's glory. The moon, the stars, the uncountable lights scattered across the night remind us that the universe is the work of His hands, shaped with a care so delicate it's described as the touch of His fingers. Standing beneath that endless canopy, we can't help but feel the wonder of it all, and the humbling question rises in us: how is it that the One who set galaxies in motion is also mindful of us?

Everywhere we look, the earth is alive with His imagination. The mountains, the oceans, the creatures that fill the land and sea — each one speaks in its own way, revealing the wisdom woven into the world. Nature becomes a teacher if we're willing to listen: the animals, the fields, the very ground beneath our feet all whisper the same truth, that everything around us bears the imprint of its Maker. And in that realization, we're invited into awe — a recognition of God's immense power, His boundless creativity, and his intimate presence in every corner of creation. And he's standing right next to you.

Psalm 8:3–4
Psalm 19:1
Psalm 104:24
Isaiah 40:26
Job 12:7–9

10

THE
INVITATION

I didn't write this book to impress anyone. I didn't write it to argue theology with anyone. I didn't write it to convert, convince, or pressure anyone either.

I wrote this because in my daily conversations with God, he said I needed to publish this one first. So, I am doing that; because being in a jungle sucks; and someone out there, maybe it's you, has felt a similar quiet pull to do something too.

This sense of — there's more. The sense of something is speaking to you. The sense that the world is not as flat or as random as it appears. The sense that the kingdom Jesus spoke of is not far away at all; but is literally inside of you right now, within your reach.

This book is not a map. It is a doorway — Into this same inner world I stepped through, back in 1986 and exactly that world as Jesus described it when He said:

"The kingdom of heaven is within you."

A world that becomes visible when the old self is left behind and a new awareness is born. One where prayer is not a ritual, but an ongoing conversation you have, with our Father in heaven. Where faith is not belief, it's an absolute knowingness aligned with every word Jesus spoke. Where authority is not ego — but your true God given identity.

36

Where the kingdom… is not a destination but a state of being your authentic self, walking…. with God in every moment of your existence. Unless you deny him, then that would be unforgivable.

I'm not asking you to believe my story…. I'm inviting you to recognize your own. Because that spark is already inside of you. It has always been there.

How many times did I see this, over and over again throughout my life? Going to church, talking with friends, studying it for years. I had an enormous library of knowledge stored in my mind. Witnesses shared it with me, Sunday school lessons taught it to me, year after ever-loving year. Countless seminars, guest speakers, missionaries, and my own in-depth study of all of it. And still, that knowledge just sat there on the counter like a three-day-old donut and a cup of stale coffee.

God literally had to pack me up, move me to the other side of the planet, drop me in a jungle, and unplug me from every distraction in my life. How dense was I. He showed me every possible way imaginable. I was diligently studying it, but completely immersed in the world — blind, no… oblivious — to what he was trying to tell me. When I say God is patient, that word doesn't even begin to express the depth of it. Not even close. God is immense Love, and every attribute of that multiplied by infinity.

Honestly, had he not moved me halfway around the world, I might never have truly seen it. It took a complete disconnection from every outside distraction for me to finally understand. And once my mind was clear, I was ready — truly ready — to see it with clarity.

As you consider your own path, the one you think you've chosen all by yourself; how many times has God shown you mercy, love, and his endless enduring patience. Are you at a thousand yet, or did you blow past that number a few decades ago.

When your moment of truth comes — whether it's in a jungle, a quiet room, a crisis or a whisper, you will know. The kingdom of heaven… opens instantaneously. All you have to do is step into it. Not drag your — old self into it and see how it smells; but you literally jump into it with every ounce of your existence, 100% all in or not, simple as that. You either do it, or take whatever it dishes out next.

11

VERSES THAT CARRIED ME

Verses I've Carried
In My Heart

God wove his words into me long before the jungle. When eve-rything collapsed and the kingdom revealed itself. Now I invite you, to reflect on these verses yourself.

Prov 7:3 "Keep My words in your heart."

Prov 4:7 "Seek wisdom first, and get understanding."

Matt 6:33 "Seek the kingdom first, and all these things will be added unto you."

Luke 17:21 "The kingdom of God is inside of you."

John 3:3 "Except a man be born again you cannot enter."

Matt 7:7 "Ask, and it shall be given…"

John 1:1 "In the beginning was the Word, and it is God."

Luke 4:32 "Speaking power and authority to command."

Matt 17:21 "none of these unless prayer and fasting first."

James 4:8 "Draw near to God, He will draw near to you"

Psalms 23:4 "As I walk through the valley, you're with me.

Psalms 52:2 "Your tongue plots destruction…"

Prov 26:28 "A false tongue hates a clean heart."

Prov 21:23 "Guard your tongue."

Read the verses and write your own reflection here.

Keep My words
In Your Heart

Walking through that gross jungle… on the third day, lost in every natural sense…, but strangely steady inside. This verse rose up in me like a memory — I didn't know I still carried. There was no noise from the outside world, no signal, no map, no path, just the sound of our footsteps and the thick breath of the jungle pressing in around us. And in that silence, these words came back to me from childhood, as if they had been waiting for this exact moment.

I remembered as a boy I read and re-read scriptures, but not really understanding them fully. I was memorizing them because I was told they mattered. Out there — In a jungle with nothing familiar to hold onto., they became something different. They weren't just words anymore. They were comfortable, peaceful present reminders, that the Creator was walking with me, and that I didn't need to fear anything in this world.

It felt like a gentle hand on my shoulder; steady, calming and anchoring. I wasn't worried about my safety, not afraid. I felt accompanied and guided. It felt like… I was learning the meaning behind the verses in real time, not from a book, but from experience itself.

That's when I understood the difference between knowing wisdom and really applying it. Between memorizing words and having them alive inside of you. Between reading the truth and walking in it.

Those words became my lifeline — not because I was in danger, but because they reminded me of who was with me. They centered me mentally and spiritually — grounding me into reality. Opening my eyes to what was happening around me, not just that jungle — but the much deeper world beneath it. And in that moment… I realized something simple and profound. Some truths don't reveal themselves until you need them.

Words I keep in my heart

____

____

____

____

____

____

SEEK WISDOM
AND GET UNDERSTANDING

By the time that verse rose up in me — we had already been walking for hours. It was the first day… we realized we were truly lost. The jungle had swallowed — the trail behind us, and every direction looked the same… dense, endless, indifferent. We were exhausted, confused… and too drained to talk. So, we stopped, sat in the thick heat, and let the silence settle in around us.

That's when this verse came back to me — not as something I had memorized, but as something alive.

"Seek wisdom first, and get understanding."

I had always known these words — but out there…, they meant something different. Knowledge was not going to get me out of that jungle. Facts… weren't going to guide my next step. Everything — I thought I knew… about the world had limits and I had reached all of them., wisdom was something else. Because without understanding it's not that useful.

Sitting there — I realized wisdom wasn't outside of me. It wasn't in some book or a plan or even strategy. It was something the Creator had placed inside me long before I ever stepped foot into a jungle.

And understanding was not something you think your way into. It's practical and something revealed when you're quiet enough to listen and apply it.

When that verse surfaced, it brought clarity, a shift and a settling. It reminded me that wisdom comes when you ask for it, when you open yourself to it…, when you stop trying to control everything and let the deeper truth rise to the surface. And in that moment., I leaned into it. I let it guide me. I let it show me what I couldn't see… on my own.

That's when the meaning of all these verses finally made sense. Wisdom's not about knowing more. It is all about seeing clearly. It's about understanding — that moment you're in. Not the one you wish you were in…. It's about letting the Creator speak through the quiet places inside of you. In the Kingdom.

And in that stillness… surrounded by the vastness of the jungle, I understood wisdom is always available. You just have to ask.

Seek

THE KINGDOM FIRST

By the third day in the jungle., everything around us felt uncertain. We had been walking — for such a long time that the hours blurred together, and the realization that we were truly lost had settled in. The jungle…, was vast, alive., and indifferent to our presence — every direction looked the same. Every sound echoing, deeper than the last. And in the middle of that exhaustion and confusion this verse rose up in me — with a clarity I had not felt in years.

"Seek the kingdom first…"

It wasn't a rebuke or guilt; it was a steady gentle honest reminder. I realized that so many of the problems, situations and circumstances in my life., had been shaped by the fact that., I wasn't seeking the kingdom first — I was seeking solutions, control and outcomes, not a kingdom.

Out there stripped of everything familiar, the meaning of that verse opened up in a way I'd not seen before… It wasn't about religion. It wasn't about behavior. It wasn't about learning anything. It was about alignment, and remembering where clarity comes from. It's about turning inward to the place where the Creator speaks to us.

When that verse surfaced, something shifted inside me. The verses that had been popping into my mind started to organize themselves… almost like they were lining up in the order…, they were meant to be understood. They weren't random memories anymore, they're connected. They were showing me the pattern. They were revealing a deeper truth.

Seeking the kingdom first., wasn't about some pie in the sky of escaping some gross jungle., It was about seeking, listening and seeing clearly…. *in* the jungle. It was about understanding a moment I was in, not the one I wished I was in. It was about letting…, Creator re-order thoughts, fears, assumptions and my understanding. Surrender.!

And in that moment, I leaned into it, letting the meaning settle. I let the truth rearrange me… from the inside out. That's when I understood something simple. When you seek the kingdom first — everything else finds its place.

THE KINGDOM OF GOD
IS INSIDE OF YOU

I was walking.... through the jungle when this verse rose up in me., not as some memory but as a realization. The heat, the weight of the air, the endless green pressing in from every direction — none of it felt threatening. It felt like a backdrop..., something was unfolding inside of me in that moment..., I understood something I'd never considered before. That kingdom..., was not somewhere far away. It wasn't up in the heavens..., It wasn't a stone castle with walls, gates and a moat.

It was inside of me.

That truth hit me with clarity I'd never experienced. I saw it in my mind's eye — not as imagination, but as recognition of a place where I could go and ask in peace, where answers rose up, not from fear or logic; but from something deeper. Something was placed there, long before I ever stepped into that jungle.

Up until that moment, I had never really understood the depth of that verse. I had read it. I had heard it. I had repeated it. But I had never *seen* it myself. And when it revealed itself, it was comforting, inspiring, and strangely invigorating. It felt like discovering a doorway that had been inside of me my entire life, waiting to be noticed.

That was the beginning., of my aha moment — the shift from knowing…. to understanding, from belief to experience. It was the moment I realized…. the Creator wasn't distant. He wasn't out there somewhere he's, right here walking with me, speaking through quiet places… inside of my own being.

And once I saw that,
everything else began to change.

Except

A MAN BE BORN AGAIN

That night in the jungle., lying there in the darkness with the sounds of the rainforest surrounding us...., this verse rose up in me with a force I wasn't expecting. The jungle is not quiet at night... it's alive, loud and constant. Inside of me there was a deep peace settling in, and the verses that had been coming to mind throughout the day were still echoing inside me, and this one came with a clarity that felt different.

"Except a man be born again..."

I had heard those words for my entire life... but honestly couldn't wrap my head around it — but out there., they took on their — true meaning. I was not thinking about physical life and death or about heaven, as some distant place. I was thinking about awareness about the way my mind was shifting the way my perception was changing. The way something inside of me was waking up.

As I lay there listening to the jungle, I realized that being born again — wasn't about starting over in the physical sense. It was about being reborn in the way you think, the way you see, the way you understand. It was a spiritual awakening and mental re-set of a new way of being present in the world.

And in that moment, I understood something I had said myself when I was seven years old, but in a way I never had before. It wasn't about religion, or some ritual. It was about stepping into a new awareness, a new clarity, a new understanding of the world around me and a world within me.

That realization changed everything and gave me a new way to see the circumstances we were in. It gave me a new way to move through them. It gave me a new way to understand the verses that were rising up inside of me and how to apply that to our reality.

It was profound but not dramatic, not loud, but deeply real experience. A quiet rebirth happening in the middle of a jungle, completely soaked by the rain, under a sky I couldn't see and surrounded by noises I couldn't identify. Being guided by a peace I couldn't explain. And from that moment on, I was never the same again.

ASK
AND IT SHALL BE GIVEN

As we moved through the jungle…, I noticed something I hadn't seen before. Every time I had a real need… it was met. Not instantly or dramatically, but quietly., naturally, almost as if the jungle itself was responding. I had been praying the whole time., walking with the Creator in my thoughts without realizing it, I was asking "praying" And every time I asked, something shifted around me.

I remember thinking how nice it would be to find a place that was dry, clean, protected — somewhere with dense trees overhead, somewhere that felt safe. And then., almost without effort., we would come upon exactly that. A clearing with a shelter of branches. That felt prepared for us., It wasn't a coincidence or luck., It was alignment. It had been happening., since the first day, but I didn't fully recognize it until the fourth. That's when this verse surfaced in my mind with clarity that stopped me in my tracks.

"Ask, and it shall be given…"

Not as a promise from a book — but as something I was living. Something unfolding right in front of me, it felt inspiring comforting and enlightening.

It brought back memories., of other times in my life when I had asked quietly and sincerely and then received exactly what I needed. But never with the sight., I had at that moment. Never with the awareness., that the Creator was walking with me, step by step, listening to every thought… every need and every whisper of my heart.

It was empowering…, in the humblest way possible. Not power over anything, but the realization — that I wasn't alone. That the Creator had my back., I could ask from a place of trust not fear and that the answers didn't come from the outside world they all rose up., from within me through the same presence that had been with me guiding me since childhood.

I finally understood…, something that's simply profound. Asking isn't about desperation…, It's about relationships and trust. It's about knowing he's listening.

And in that jungle, I knew.

IN THE BEGINNING
WAS THE WORD

By the morning of the fifth day everything inside me had shifted. I had not eaten…, for several days and our water was almost gone. My body was weak, but my awareness had never been sharper. I was walking through that jungle in a state that felt… both physical and spiritual at the same time; fasting by circumstance., and praying without stopping, and feeling the Creator beside me… with a presence so real it felt tangible.

I couldn't reach out and touch him…., but I felt him with every step. In that state of exhaustion, emptiness and open, this verse rose up inside with a vibration I still feel forty years later.

"In the beginning was the Word
and the Word is God."

I had heard this my whole life, but out there it wasn't a verse. It was true and powerful…. the foundation behind everything I was experiencing. Because…, I had realized something simple and profound.

The WORDS WE SPEAK shape the world we experience.

Not in some mystical magical way; but in a deeply real and practical way.

Tom and I were speaking things out loud about what we needed and what we hoped for, what we were looking for and then… we were stepping directly into those things. Over and over…, day after day. It was not a coincidence. It was not my imagination. It was an obvious alignment.

The Word is God; meaning the creative force behind everything is carried in the words we speak…, the thoughts we hold, the intentions we set. In that jungle I saw it happen repeatedly, in real time. I saw how every request, every need…, every quiet prayer was being met. I saw how the Creator was responding not from the outside… but from within.

That realization hit deeply, it changed everything. It was the moment the entire experience shifted from survival to revelation. I understood that the very same presence walking beside me was the very same presence… speaking through me. The same presence that had been guiding me since childhood. And once I saw that... the verses that had been rising up inside me weren't just memories anymore. They were instructions. They were… the truth. They were the blueprint; inside the kingdom I was stepping into. And from that moment on I walked differently.

These verses surfaced at the exact moment when everything inside of me shifted. It wasn't loud or emotional. It wasn't dramatic, it was simply *true*.!

And once I saw it, I couldn't unsee it.

Tom and I were walking through that jungle., exhausted, hungry
and worn down by days of uncertainty and while I was experiencing spiritual awakening and clarity rising inside me, Tom sank
deeper…, into pretty dark thoughts. The opposite of my experience. He spoke something out loud that was all negative, surren-
dering to circumstances. He wasn't trying to harm us., he was
simply an overwhelmed human., tired and done.

But the moment those words left his mouth, something in me
recognized the danger of them, not physically, but spiritually. Because I had already begun., to see how our words were shaping.,
our experience. I had already seen how every request…, every
need, every quiet prayer was being met. I had already seen how
the Creator was walking with me, responding to these intentions
rising inside of my heart. And when Tom…, spoke a negative
thought, this verse instantly hit the front of my mind, with absolute clarity:

Not authority over the jungle, or authority over another person. But authority over my own intentions — words. Authority over my own world. Authority over the reality I was stepping into. None of this was religious. It wasn't mystical. It wasn't emotional. It was simply the truth revealing itself.

All these verses that had been coming to mind one after another, day after day suddenly connected like pieces of a giant puzzle. These weren't random memories…, they were instructions, showing me how the kingdom works. How creation works through intention… and how the inner world shapes the outer one…. and in that moment, I took charge of the situation not by force or fear… but by speaking with the authority the Creator placed inside of me from the beginning. I used the Word to create a path forward… with intention to shape the next step — I used the truth rising inside of me, to guide us out of that jungle.

That was the moment this major shift happened and the moment when everything aligned. When I'd understood what had been true all along. From that point… I walked with a different awareness, not of power, but of partnership. Not of control but alignment. Not fear., but authority rooted in the Creator Himself.

This Comes Only By Prayer and Fasting First

When this verse surfaced… it wasn't a reminder it was a realization. A recognition of understanding — about all I had been going through and feeling without trying., was preparation.

By the time this verse rose up in me… I had not eaten in days. My body was empty, but my awareness was sharp. I had been walking — in constant conversation with God Creator; not formal prayer or ritual, but a steady ongoing dialogue. An understanding — with clarity., about who he is and who I am. And without planning it, without intending to, I had been fasting…, not by choice, but by circumstances. I realized something profound, it's only by stepping into alignment, that we can reach these certain levels of understanding. Physically, mentally and spiritually, all clicking together.

It wasn't fun. It wasn't comfortable. It wasn't something I would have chosen; but it was necessary. Not because of difficulty… but because what I was about ready to see and understand — required a higher level of clarity that only comes., when the noise is stripped away and the inner world becomes unmistakably loud.

"This kind comes
only by prayer and fasting."

Not as a rule or command… but as a description of what alignment feels like. I was doing exactly what's required for what was coming, when everything shifts, the verses would connect and a logic would reveal itself. When the understanding crystallizes into something I'd never seen before. This was the doorway, the threshold. The final piece — of preparation before:

Ripple Logic Schematic
revealed itself.

It was a deeply personal moment, not religious, but real. Undeniably and profoundly true. Once I saw that, I knew what was coming next.

THE FABRIC
OF EXISTENCE REVEALED

There are moments in life that don't change you — they *redefine* you by rearranging the way you see everything. The way you understand reality around you and the way you move through it. This was that moment for me.

After days of walking., praying., fasting by circumstance, and aligning myself without even realizing it, something opened. It wasn't dramatic or emotional. It wasn't mystical, it was simply *true*, and when it happened, it was as if the veil between the seen and unseen was lifted, just enough for me to glimpse — the structure behind everything.

I saw the fabric of existence.

Not with my eyes — but with my awareness that had been sharpening day by day. I saw everything was connected. How intentions ripple outward and the Creator's design is woven into every moment, every thoughtful word. And I realized the awesome power of God who made everything intelligent, beautiful and precise. Love that's embedded into the very structure of reality. Truly profound to see. It's been a life long journey, to really fully comprehend it.

**It was humbling
in the deepest sense.**

I finally understood… what I was being shown wasn't for me alone. It's an insight that comes with a responsibility. It's meant to be shared, to help lift others up. And that's when Ripple Logic was born. Not as idea or theory alone but as revelation. A schematic for seeing how our inner world shapes the outer one, how intention, experience, and alignment create movement., at a level that's taken decades to unpack it, into what has become multiple series of writing. In many different genres, because everything exists within this.

Walking through every day of my life since, with that insight has been a blessing., beyond anything I could have imagined. Allowing me to help thousands of people around the world. It has become the very fountain from which hundreds of applications were used, each one improving the lives of the people it touches.

All of it traces back to that moment in the jungle, when the Creator opened my eyes to a structure beneath everything and trusted me with the responsibility of carrying it forward to humanity.

Ripple Logic didn't come from me… It came *through* me. And it continues rippling outward, touching lives in ways I could have never predicted or ever know of.

MEMORIZE THIS

These words changed my life forever
In the middle of a jungle.

"Keep My words in your heart, seek wisdom first and get understanding, seek the kingdom first…, and all of these things will be added unto you. The kingdom of God is inside of you, except a man be born again., you cannot enter. Ask and it shall be given you. In the beginning…, was the Word, the Word is God, speaking power and authority to command. None of these unless prayer and fasting first. Draw near to God, he will draw near to you. Though I walk through the valley… you are with me. Your tongue plots destruction. False tongues hate a clean heart. God is always faithful to us."

"In the beginning was the Word — and the Word was with God — and the Word was God. Keep My words in your heart. Seek wisdom first. The Kingdom is inside of you. Ask and it shall be given. Speak with authority. First pray and fast. Draw near unto me and I will draw near to you. Even in the valley I am with you. Guard your tongue. I am faithful."

12

What Happened
A Reflection

It's been forty years since that moment in the jungle, the collapse and detonation of my awakening. And even now, when I think back on it… the feeling is as fresh as if it happened yesterday. Not because of chasing any old experience. But because the truth I stepped into that day has never left me. It became the foundation for the walk I am still on. The lens I see through. The quiet knowing that guides every breath… of my life. Many people often ask what changed for me after that moment and the answer is quite simple: **EVERYTHING** instantly.

The light of God… created a glow from within me. Not a life free of challenges. Because the world outside stayed the same. **I changed,** my awareness and perceptions all changed. My understanding of God and myself changed. I realized the kingdom — Jesus spoke about — is exactly where he said it is. Not some far-off place, or reward for good behavior. It wasn't a destination after death. It is a living reality inside of us — Right now, right here, in this present moment.

The kingdom responds to aligned intentions, and it is a kingdom… that listens to every word uttered from your heart and lips. A kingdom that moves in alignment with God's creative force.

Once you see this, you can't unsee it.

I've spent decades watching this…, how it works in my life and in the lives of others in the quiet patterns of the world. And how truth…., is always the same. The inner kingdom is what shapes the outer world. The kingdom within us… is shaping the life we walk through. Not because we're so powerful. Because God has designed us that way from the beginning. Genesis wasn't poetry. It's identity. Jesus wasn't giving us religion, not at all.

He was teaching us how to do this.

And that moment in the jungle — the collapse, and detonation, the rebirth, it was simply a moment when I had listened to the knowingness… and understood what was true all along. I didn't earn this and I certainly didn't deserve it. And honestly, I didn't know what I was stepping into. But God knew…. he had been preparing me for this since the time I was born.

You've read this far… maybe you're being prepared for a life defining moment and collapse and awakening to the doorway into the kingdom yourself… and when it comes whether quietly or violently…, whether in a whisper or a storm you'll know. Truth has a way of recognizing itself.

Peace, Love, and Light

James

Reflection on my own life.

____

____

____

____

____

____

____

____

____

____

Legacy Moment

13

THE STORY BEGINS IN THE BIBLE

In the Beginning

"In the beginning…, God created the heavens and the earth." Genesis 1:1 The Bible opens with…, God who creates not out of boredom or necessity, but out of intention and love. That first sentence sets the tone for everything that follows.

Wisdom is the first quality we see in God's work. Creation isn't chaotic; it's ordered, purposeful, and beautifully interconnected.

Power is evident in the scale of creation, from galaxies to grains of sand.

Justice appears as God's commitment to what is right. He cares about fairness and truth.

Mercy balances justice. God is patient, offering forgiveness and every second chance. You have limited time to decide.

Love ties everything together — steady, faithful, and deeply relational to everyone and things in creation.

These are tenants I've learned throughout the entirety of my journey up to this moment. And this is the foundation upon which the rest of the story stands upon.

Human Condition

"God created man in his own image…" Genesis 1:27

This is the verse that grants us the authority and power to create by choice, *by free will*, as God has designed us to do.

Right after introducing God, the Bible introduces us, and it does so with remarkable dignity.

Identity is the starting point. Being made in God's image gives every person inherent worth and power.

Creativity reflects that image. Humans imagine, build, design, and dream.

Morality is part of our design too, — an inner sense of right and wrong.

Conflict (Sin) enters when our desires pull us in different directions from what God intended for us.

Brokenness is the honest conclusion: we're capable of great good, but also great harm. Including ourselves and people around us.

Old World

"For all — have sinned… and come short of the glory of God." Romans 3:23 If humans were made good, why does it seem like the world is so impossibly difficult and fractured? The Bible's answer is simple… sin is choosing our way instead of God's and it creates a ripple effect that touches everything you experience.

Separation is the first consequence — from God, from others, and even from ourselves.

Disorder follows that separation.

Injustice becomes a symptom of that disorder.

Emptiness settles in when we try to fill the spiritual gap with things that can't be satisfied.

Longing remains — a quiet reminder that life was meant to be more abundant and whole.

14

Bible Study Before The Jungle

Human Condition

1. God's posture toward humanity is forgiveness

2. The human condition {Romans 3:23

3. The consequence {Romans 6:23

4. The rescue {John 3:16

5. Ongoing repentance {1 John 1:9

6. Repentance is refreshing {Acts 3:19

7. The heart posture God responds to {Psalm 51:17

8. The spiritual battle after salvation {James 4:7–8

9. Transformation and renewal {Romans 12:1–2

10. Identity in Christ {Galatians 2:20

11. Rebirth of sight — the kingdom within {John 3:3

12. Conclusion "Repentance brings us into the kingdom of God, from within."

"I will be their God, and they shall be my people."
Jeremiah 31:33

Here's where the story takes a surprising turn. God has not walked away. He loves all that live in his truth. Our calling begins as we feel the connection, like my own experience. Covenant is the structure…., of that relationship. God's promise of faithfulness. Guidance comes through the quiet still voice from within us. Patience defines God's dealings with humanity and His promise anchors his words and the expectation of a new world within us, and that is reality created.

Legacy Moment

1. The Human Condition Needs Rescue

Romans 3:23 "For all have sinned and come short of the glory of God." This explains John 3:16 and why we need his salvation. By naming the human condition — and the universal brokenness. This brings the gospel together.

Romans 6:23 "For the wages of sin is death; but the gift of God is eternal life through Jesus Christ our Lord." This verse is the entire Bible in two halves. The problem "the wages of sin is death" The solution…, "the gift of God is eternal life through Jesus Christ" It's the gospel story in one breath.

Together they form the Bible's foundation:

1. The Need - Romans 3:23 Humanity is broken.

2. The Consequence — Romans 6:23
   Sin against God's design for us leads to death.

3. The Rescue — John 3:16 God intervenes with love, sacrifice, alignment and restoration.

Everything else in Scripture, all the prophets, the poetry, and the letters expands…, illustrates and supports these truths. They are the spine of the gospel story.

Legacy Moment

2. Repentance, Cleansing, and Returning to God

1 John 1:9 — The "Ongoing Repentance" Verse This is the verse that explains what a believer does after salvation: "If we confess our sins… he is faithful and just to forgive us our sins, and to cleanse our unrighteousness." This is the "daily washing." The maintenance of the soul. The answer to: How do I repent, when I mess up again?" It's not about earning salvation again, it's about restoring the fellowship, and practicing what we've learned. This verse is a lifeline.

Acts 3:19 — The Repentance, Refreshing Verse" "Repent ye therefore, and be converted, that your sins may be blotted out, when times of refreshing shall come from the presence of the Lord, filling you…., repentance isn't punishment. It's refreshing. It's spiritual oxygen. An entirely new world emerged for me, instantly.! The truth is, you need to talk with God every day. All day is better.!

Psalm 51:17 — "God Responds to Brokenness" "A broken and a contrite heart, O God, thou wilt not despise." This is the verse that answers: "How do I repent if I don't know the right words?" God isn't looking for perfect language. He's looking for… a soft heart, like I had in a jungle. This verse is a spiritual key.

Legacy Moment

3. The Battle After Salvation

James 4:7–8 — "Spiritual Resistance" Verses "Submit yourselves therefore to God. Resist the devil, and he will flee from you." "Draw near to God, and he will draw near to you." These are really jaw dropping when you finally realize what they mean: Repentance is submission to God's authority and power. Temptation is., resistance to alignment. Closeness to God is alignment. The enemy runs from spiritual authority, not fear. Like Tom stopped speaking evil against our own survival. These verses explain the battle that begins when we accept God.

My own battles

____

____

____

____

____

____

Legacy Moment

My own battles

Legacy Moment

4. Transformation and the New Identity

Romans 12:1–2 — The "Transformation" "Give all of yourself to God." And be transformed… by the renewing of your mind. This verse explains why., the ego-mind claws and fights with you — because your salvation is instant — but transformation is ongoing. Forty years… as I count my own — and each moment., has been with free will to choose…, good or bad. These verses describe the process.

Romans 12:1–2 — The Identity Shifting, Life Reorienting Passage… These verses don't just teach repentance, they transform the entire inner world…, of a person who has just been saved. They speak directly to the ego mind digging in its heels, the battle between… the old self and the new self and the question of "what now? — There is a process of becoming someone different. We have to surrender to God, for him to lead us to actual change. Renewal of the mind rewires the soul. This is the moment where salvation becomes transformation. This is the moment where belief becomes identity. This is the moment where the old self dies and the new self-rises. This is the moment where the soul says: "I'm not who I was anymore."

What has changed in me

Legacy Moment

In my own experience the moment of ending and beginning, decision, power and authority that is exactly a spiritual earthquake…, written about in:

Romans 12:1–2. It's not gentle. It's a powerful verse. It's a surgical verse. It cuts the old self away entirely and reveals the new.

Galatians 2:20 — The "I Am Not That Person Anymore" Verse This is the verse that explains the death of my old self and what the birth of the new is. This is the verse that hits with power and authority when someone is standing at the edge of their old life. This is the verse that says: "The old me is totally gone, and God lives in me now." This verse shows us how salvation converts us through our new identity. And surrender into strength. Repentance to rebirth. The broken into a new creation. And the moment I experienced in a jungle is exactly a

Galatians 2:20 moment.

____

____

____

____

____

🫀 Legacy Moment

Let this moment live in your words.

5. The Revelation of Sight - The Kingdom Within

"Except a man be born again, he cannot see the kingdom of God." (John 3:3) Not "enter." Not "reach." Not "arrive." **See**

That's the part most people miss. Jesus wasn't talking about a location. He wasn't talking about a future afterlife. He wasn't talking about some moral checklist. He was talking about perception. A new consciousness. A new awareness. A new inner world. A rebirth of sight. Real power and authority.

And when that hits you — like it did with me, in a jungle, in the heat, in the fear, in the collapse of an old world — it wasn't some bible thumping religious doctrine. It was a detonation. Brutal and Raw.

Because the moment I saw the truth my old world died. And this new one erupted. That's why this journal reads like a cosmic implosion. Because that's exactly what spiritual rebirth feels like when it's not softened by religion or ritual. It's not gentle. It's not symbolic. It's not poetic. It's violent and absolute. It's identity shattering. It leaves you standing in a world that is the same... but you are not.

That verse didn't just speak to me. It rewired me. It fused my awareness into the architecture of reality with the same resonance I've been articulating..., forty years.

The same current that shaped Ripple Logic is., the same force that has been guiding my life and instincts ever since. I didn't just learn a few Scriptures." I was reborn with them inside of me. And that's why nothing has ever been the same.

Repentance brings us the kingdom of God, from within, exactly the way Jesus brought us the Gospel.

Let this moment live in your words.

____

____

____

____

____

____

____

____

Legacy Moment

JESUS

"For God so loved the world, that he gave his only begotten Son…" — John 3:16 When you reach the New Testament, the story sharpens into focus.

Revelation is what Jesus brings — a clear picture of God in human form. Like God created us to be.

Compassion marks His interactions.

Teaching forms the heart of His ministry.

Sacrifice of our own ego-mind becomes the turning point — the healing of that separation.

Hope rises with everything Jesus taught us. For it is not religion, it is certainly the most life changing message that exists in this world. It's been taught by many wise people for eons of time. The truth is undeniable.

More on this in the next Ripple Ministry Series book.

15

PRAYER OF SALVATION

If something in your heart feels drawn towards God and you long for the peace of mind, forgiveness and a fresh start, and the knowing that God is…, the power and authority over everything. The Bible says… God is already reaching toward you. Then say this… in your heart, mind and mouth with absolute knowing that God is always listening to you.

GOD

I come to you through your son Jesus

I come to You just as I am.

I confess that I have sinned and I ask for Your forgiveness.

I believe in your power and authority and promise… to forgive me of my sins, and create a new me.

I open my heart and accept you as my God, Savior and Lord of my life.

Make me new, and help me to walk with you from this day forward and for the rest of my life.

Amen.”

Scripture “For whosoever shall call upon the name of the Lord shall be saved.” — **Romans 10:13**

What Changed Inside of me at this moment.

____

TRANSFORMED LIFE

"Be ye transformed by the renewing of your mind..." Romans 12:2 The Bible doesn't just tell a story it... invites us into it.

Renewal begins on the inside.

Love becomes the guiding principle.

Forgiveness frees us from all bitterness.

Humility reshapes how we see ourselves.

Purpose emerges as we align with God's vision.

THE NEW WORLD

"Behold, I make all things new." Revelation 21:5 The Bible doesn't end with escape it ends with renewal.

Restoration is the final promise.

Healing touches every level of life.

Justice is finally complete.

Presence is restored — God with His people.

Newness defines the ending.

THE THREAD

If you had to — summarize the Bible's message… in
one sweeping arc it might sound like this.

God made us
and we have wandered off.

He continues to be with us.

Jesus brought us salvation
to restore us.

And one day
everything broken will be made whole.

That is the heartbeat of Scripture,
the "most important knowledge" it offers.

My Promise to God and Myself.

____

____

____

____

____

____

____

____

____

Legacy Moment

CLOSING PRAYER

Father, thank you for the quiet work you do in my heart, the healing no one sees, and your strength that rises up slowly, with hope that returns like the morning light.

For the one reading these words…, surround them with your peace. Let your presence… steady their steps, and your love calm their fears and your promises renew their hope.

When their heart feels heavy, be their refuge and when their path feels uncertain, be their guide, their strength and their source.

And as they move forward, may they discover again and again that you are near, you are faithful, and you make all things new.

Amen.

Scripture *"Hope thou in God…"* — Psalm 42:11

16

EPILOGUE

Over the past 40 years, I've had time — and experience to reflect on what happened during that life-changing moment. I've traveled the world, studied every renowned spiritual work I could find, searching for the one overarching truth that resonates across all of them.

The Bible is the one I grew up with. It's the one I know best. But what I discovered is that the same truth lives inside of all of the great spiritual writings I've studied. There is one Creator. And God is the name I know Him by.

Through all the stories, parables, and mental illustrations across all traditions — the most important thing I learned is this:

God is real.

He created Absolutely
Everything.

And when we keep those thoughts in our hearts and minds, when we hold those truths as daily tenants of our life; we begin to see the deeper meaning behind every little and big thing we experience.

Without that awareness, life can feel confusing, disconnected. We find ourselves asking, *"What does it all mean?"*

But when we hold respect for the Creator, He is always faithful to show us whatever we are seeking.

In *The Jungle Gospel*, I've detailed those events as I experienced them — and how I came to understand the wisdom God showed me. Had I not memorized those snippets of verses, I might never have gained the wisdom of those words. I might never have conceived the understanding that those verses are not just ideas they are:

Actions that cause **effects** change with real **transformation**.

What Actions did I create an Effect with

____

____

____

____

____

____

Keep My Words in Your Heart

This verse is the root from which the entire path of my life has grown. I learned early on that knowledge is necessary for everything we face in life — and that spiritual knowledge is the highest form of it. Who else could possibly teach me more than the Creator Himself, through the inspired words he gave to people across time?

When I studied those words, they rang true through my whole being — mind, heart, body, and spirit. That resonance was how I knew they were genuine. The truth didn't come from someone telling me it was true; it came from the way it resonated inside of me as I experienced them.

So, I took it at face value. I held onto the verses that resonated, the ones that felt honest and alive. I memorized them because they were real to me. They were the foundation I carried into every moment that followed.

SEEK WISDOM FIRST

When I first heard this verse as a child, I honestly had no idea what it meant — but I understood that it mattered. Something in me knew it was important, even if I couldn't explain why. So, I did the only thing I knew how to do: I started reading. I went to the one book I trusted, the one that felt true and honest inside me.

I even asked the librarian — when my mom took me there who the wisest person in the world was. She handed me books about people I had never heard of, from cultures and times I didn't understand. As a child, it was confusing. I was searching for wisdom, but I didn't yet know what wisdom looked like.

So, I asked people in my life. Several of them said Solomon was the wisest person they knew of. That made me smile, because I had heard of him before. So, I began studying what he had to say.

He wrote that we should spend all our resources to get wisdom and that above all else, we should get understanding. I still didn't fully grasp what that meant, but I remembered it. I held onto it. I carried it with me because I knew it was important, even if the meaning hadn't fully opened up yet.

And that simple act of remembering, it was the beginning of everything that followed.

Legacy Moment

This verse didn't make sense to me at first. As a kid, I thought learning was just remembering things. But sitting at home doing homework with my mom, I began to see what "understanding" really meant.

She would ask, "What did you learn today?" I'd repeat the facts I remembered. Then she'd ask, "What does that mean?" So, I'd think about it — reflect on how it connected to something I already knew.

But then came the real question:
"How do you actually use that, to do something?"

That's where understanding began to take shape for me. It wasn't just knowing something or even being wise about it. It was the moment when knowledge and wisdom turned into *action*, when something you learned caused a real effect in the world.

Sometimes the practical steps weren't obvious. Sometimes I had to experiment, try things, or build little models to show my mom how it worked. But that process — taking knowledge, adding wisdom, and turning it into something real — that was the full cycle Solomon talked about with understanding wisdom.

That's when I finally understood what "get understanding" meant. And it became one of the most valuable lessons of my life.

Book of Proverbs

SOLOMON WAS RIGHT.

What God has taught me

____

____

____

____

____

____

____

SEEK THE KINGDOM FIRST

When I first heard this verse as a child, I imagined a kingdom like the ones in the movies — a far-off place with walls and towers, something you could travel to if you were good enough or old enough. I didn't know what it really meant, but I knew it was important, so I tried to study it. I wanted to find out where this kingdom was, and maybe someday go there myself.

When my grandmother passed away, that's when the idea started to shift. People said she was "in heaven now," and I knew they meant the kingdom of heaven. But I had just seen her at the funeral. How could she be somewhere else? That confusion stayed with me.

So, I asked the one person who was always honest and sincere with me — my mom. She told me the kingdom of heaven is inside of us. I remember scratching my head, thinking.,

> *How can a whole kingdom be inside me?*
> It made no sense at all.

I asked her to show me where it said that in the Bible, and she did. She explained it the best she could, and even though I didn't fully understand it, I now knew where to look for answers. The confusion didn't disappear, but the verse stayed with me:

**Seek the kingdom of heaven,
seek the kingdom of God — first,
and everything else will be added to you.**

I thought about the things Jesus did — the fish, the wine, the loaves of bread, all the illustrations he gave. Those stories comforted me after losing my grandmother. They made me feel more confident that this kingdom was real, even if I didn't yet understand how, it could be "inside" me.

I wasn't fully certain of that part — not until the moment in the jungle, when everything finally made sense.

My Continuous Conversation with God.

Except a Man Be Born Again

I first said those words when I was seven years old, sitting on the couch with my mom one summer afternoon. The big window was open, the air was cool, and birds were singing on the branches just outside. Mom was cooking lunch in the kitchen, and I had been thinking about this for weeks maybe months.

I finally asked Mom
"How does God come live inside of me?"

She told me He had always been there, but that I had never decided to *ask* him to live there with me. I thought about that for a long time. I said, "But He's already there." She nodded and said, "Yes, but did you invite Him to be there to talk with you, to walk with you, to be yours?" I said no. She told me that was the difference.

I understood that. So, she helped me, just like I described in *The Jungle Gospel*. I said the words, and I meant them. But the true "born again" feeling — the one that transforms everything, didn't happen until that moment in the jungle.

Because in the blink of an eye, there I was, standing in the kingdom of heaven in the middle of a jungle, feeling everything, I had memorized and studied for so many years.

It was as if all those verses came alive at once. It literally felt like being born again — not just having a personal relationship with the Creator every day, but stepping into the very fabric of reality He made, the kingdom where everything is possible.

My Promise to God and Myself.

____

____

____

____

____

____

____

____

Ask and It Shall Be Given You

I learned early in life that we could ask God for whatever needs we had and that He would take care of us. At first, I did that silently in my thoughts, and later I learned how to pray in the way I was taught. But if I'm honest, that only worked a small percentage of the time, maybe five percent; because I wasn't really aligned with what God wanted for me.

Most of my prayers back then were about things I *wanted*, not things I truly *needed*. That's what it means to be out of alignment to ask from the ego instead of the spirit. And even though ego-driven prayers sometimes seem to work a little, it's only because some tiny part of them happens to line up with something deeper we can't see yet.

But in the jungle, everything was different. My needs were real. My conversations with God were real. I wasn't asking from ego anymore — I was asking from alignment, from truth, from the place inside me that was connected to His greater good for my life. And that's when this verse became clear to me.

Ask and it shall be given

That wasn't about getting what I wanted — it was about being aligned with God so that what I needed could flow naturally, moment by moment.

In that alignment every need was met.
Not all at once but exactly when it is needed.

What I Thank God for, Giving to me

____

____

____

____

____

____

____

THE WORD IS GOD

As I grew older, with the wisdom I'd learned from Solomon and many other voices in my studies, I began noticing something: when people were energized, emotional, and deeply invested in something — and they spoke about it repeatedly — those things would start happening in their lives.

They didn't understand why. They thought life was happening *to* them. But I could see they were speaking it into their own experience.

It saddened me, because many of them were creating outcomes they didn't want. But for whatever reason, they were committed to repeating those words, those emotions, those beliefs — and life responded.

That was my first glimpse of what I would later experience firsthand in the jungle.

There, with Tom, everything we said — everything we felt with sincerity and emotion — unfolded in real time. Sometimes within minutes. Sometimes within seconds. It became surreal to watch it happen, not as a theory, but as a living reality.

It was undeniable.
We were speaking it and feeling it.
And then we were living it.

In that moment, the meaning of "The Word is God" became clear. Not as a metaphor or doctrine; but as a direct experience of how reality responds to the words we speak and the emotions we carry.

We were doing it
to ourselves the entire time.

What have My own words created

____

____

____

____

____

____

____

PRAYER AND FASTING FIRST

I grew up knowing how to pray and how to walk with God moment by moment. I leaned on Him for understanding, for wisdom, for seeing why things happened the way they did. That part made sense to me. But fasting — that was the mystery. I understood the physical reasons for it, but I couldn't understand why it was spiritually important, or why some translations removed it from the Bible. That puzzled me deeply.

Matthew 17:21 made it sound like a deal-maker or a deal-breaker. I remembered the verse, but I never fully understood its significance.

Over time, I began to see that fasting wasn't about starving the body — it was about bringing the body into obedience to the spirit. It was about quieting the ego-mind with all its wants, cravings and distractions. When the body is subdued, the spirit becomes clearer. When the ego is quiet, the consciousness aligns.

Fasting creates a kind of inner resonance — spirit, mind and body all tuned to the same frequency. A perfect trifecta.

And when that alignment happens, things begin to move. Sometimes within minutes, seconds or instantaneously.

That's what Jesus was teaching.
And in the jungle, it became unmistakably clear.

There, stripped of comfort, stripped of distraction, stripped of ego, I was aligned — fully, completely. Prayer wasn't a ritual. It was a conversation. Fasting wasn't a discipline. It was a doorway. And through that doorway, the fabric of creation responded.

In that moment I finally understood
why prayer and fasting were meant to go together.

What days I Pray and Fast

____

____

____

____

____

____

____

God Is Always Faithful

Across my entire lifetime, I have learned this to be absolutely true:

God is always faithful — even when we are not.

The wisdom I found in the Bible is something I can share, but the understanding is something each person has to develop within themselves. It's an internal value, shaped by experience, and it becomes yours alone.

In the jungle, I learned more in a short span of time than I had in years. Our thoughts, our ego-mind, our emotions, and our feelings were all working against us. And yet, because I had these words stored in my heart and mind, God showed me exactly how everything was happening and how it all works inside the fabric of His creation.

I saw clearly that our own words were causing our problems. And our own words were the way out of them.

Guard your tongue — because what you say is building something. Guard your thoughts — because they outline the path that will bring things into your life, good or bad. The choice is yours. That's free will.

And through all of it, God remains faithful. He shows us the truth when we're ready to see it. He guides us when we're willing to listen. He reveals the path when our heart is aligned with Him.

In the jungle, that faithfulness became undeniable.

How God has always been faithful to me

🐾 Legacy Moment

CORE PRINCIPLES OF A JOURNEY

Keep My Words in Your Heart

Seek Wisdom First

Get Understanding

Seek the Kingdom First

Except a Man Be Born Again

Ask and It Shall Be Given You

The Word Is God

Prayer and Fasting First

God Is Always Faithful

Legacy Moment

Where my journey is taking me next.

Legacy Moment

17

THIS CHANGED ME FOREVER

IN

THE HEART

OF A JUNGLE

One truth shattered reality, a single command that rewired everything I was sure I knew. These are verses that have kept ringing in my mind, for all of these years. And that's power in the word.

"In the beginning was the word and the Word was with God and the word was/is God. Keep my words in your heart. Seek wisdom first. The Kingdom is inside of you. Ask and it shall be given. First pray and fast… then speak with authority in God's power. Draw near unto God, and he will draw near to you. Even in the valley or a jungle he's with you. Guard your tongue, because it is what causes the most harm. God is always faithful."

Thank you for helping this message reach the hands and hearts of those who need it most.

Ripple Ministry™

GOD

IS ALWAYS WITH YOU

About the Author

The creator of Ripple❤Logic™
Master trainer and developer is focused on helping people, their families and businesses grow with resilient clarity. His works provides practical applications and real transformations that resonate for generations. Solutions-based steps for building strong legacies and navigating our real-world challenges with confidence.

Learn more at:

https://ripple-logic.com

Ripple ❤ Legacy™